EDGE
BOOKS™

THE GUYS' GUIDE TO MAKING THE OUTDOORS MORE AWESOME

BY ERIC BRAUN

CAPSTONE PRESS
a capstone imprint

Edge Books are published by Capstone Press,
1710 Roe Crest Drive, North Mankato, Minnesota 56003
www.capstonepub.com

Library of Congress Cataloging-in-Publication Data
Braun, Eric, 1971–
The guys' guide to making the outdoors more awesome / by Eric Braun.
pages cm.—(Edge books. The guys' guides)
Includes bibliographical references and index.
Summary: "Describes various tips, activities, and useful information for making the
outdoors more fun and interesting"—Provided by publisher.
ISBN 978-1-4765-3922-5 (library binding)
ISBN 978-1-4765-5970-4 (ebook PDF)
1. Outdoor recreation—Juvenile literature. I. Title.
GV191.62.B73 2014
796.5—dc23   2013035407

Editorial Credits
Aaron Sautter, editor; Veronica Scott, designer; Eric Gohl, media researcher;
Jennifer Walker, production specialist

Photo Credits
Alamy: FLPA, 16 (lynx scat), Gary Cook, 16 (wolf scat), Joe Blossom, 16 (beaver
scat), Rafael Ben-Ari, 20, Simon Colmer, 16 (fox scat); BigStockPhoto.com: SURZ,
14; Capstone: 8, 9 (bottom), 10, 21; Capstone Studio: Karon Dubke, 11, 23 (fishing
rod); Getty Images: Allsport/Robert Cianflone, 15; iStockphotos: Sieto, 16 (bear scat),
Whiteway, 16 (hare scat); Library of Congress: 27 (bottom); Newscom: Splash News,
24; Shutterstock: 1973kla, 2 (top), Anatolich, 13 (cricket), attaphong, 9 (top), Attitude,
cover (bear), 2 (middle), Audrey Snider-Bell, 28 (bottom), 29 (bottom), AVA Bitter, 26
(top), Big Pants Production, 29 (top), Brandon Alms, 13 (firefly), Brian Lasenby, 12
(prickly pear), Catalin Petolea, 6 (front), Danussa, cover (landscape), Dariusz Majgier,
13 (tick), Decha Thapanya, 13 (blister beetle), Dr. Morley Read, 19 (bottom left),
fotosub, 12 (acorn), Galyna Andrushko, 4–5, geraria, 16 (illustrated fox), Hyde Peranitti,
13 (caterpillar), iko, 12 (mushroom), JENG_NIAMWHAN, 12 (wild rice), Kenneth
Keifer, 12 (hemlock), Microstock Man, 6–7, mironov, 22–23 (background), Nagy-Bagoly
Arpad, 12 (blackberries), Ortodox, 13 (maggot), PePl, 2 (bottom), Photo House, 17,
plasid, 12 (rosary peas), Potapov Alexander, 17, prizzz, 12 (baneberries), Scott E Read,
18, Seamartini Graphics, 23 (fish), Serg64, 13 (fly), Sign N Symbol Production, 28 (top),
Smileus, 12 (poisonous nuts), smuay, 13 (termite), Stealh, 13 (grasshopper), Steshkin
Yevgeniy, 13 (earthworms), Tatiana Volgutova, 12 (cattails), Tribalium, 12 (illustrated
reeds), TTphoto, 16 (moose scat), Tyler Olson, 16 (deer scat), Volodymyr Burdiak,
19 (top), yienkeat, 13 (illustrated trees), Yourthstock, 19 (bottom right); SuperStock:
Animals Animals, 16 (raccoon scat); Wikipedia: Jami Dwyer, 25, Public Domain, 26
(bottom), 27 (top)

Design Elements: Shutterstock

Printed in the United States of America in Stevens Point, Wisconsin.
092013   007768WZS14

TABLE OF CONTENTS

MAKE YOUR OWN ADVENTURE

Have you ever dreamed of going on an outdoor adventure? Out in the wild, you can slash your way through the underbrush while finding your way by the stars. You can forage for food and water using nothing but your wits. If you encounter a wild animal, you can stare it down and have a great story to share with your friends.

forage—to search for food

Modern life can be pretty sweet. It's fun to order pizza and play video games on the couch. But the most incredible adventures aren't found in your living room—they're found in the outdoors. And you don't need to head to the mountains or a jungle to find them. Read on to discover how awesome the outdoors can be. Learn how to build a survival shelter. Find out how to recognize animal signs or what to do if you become lost. If you're curious, brave, and prepared, there's no limit to the amazing experiences you can have in the great outdoors!

MAKE HIKES FUN

Hiking is a great, fun way to experience the outdoors. Hiking costs very little, and it can be an awesome adventure if you plan ahead. Going with a couple of friends can make your hike safer and a lot more fun. Bring along a cell phone in case of an emergency. And stay on marked trails to avoid getting lost—which wouldn't be much fun at all.

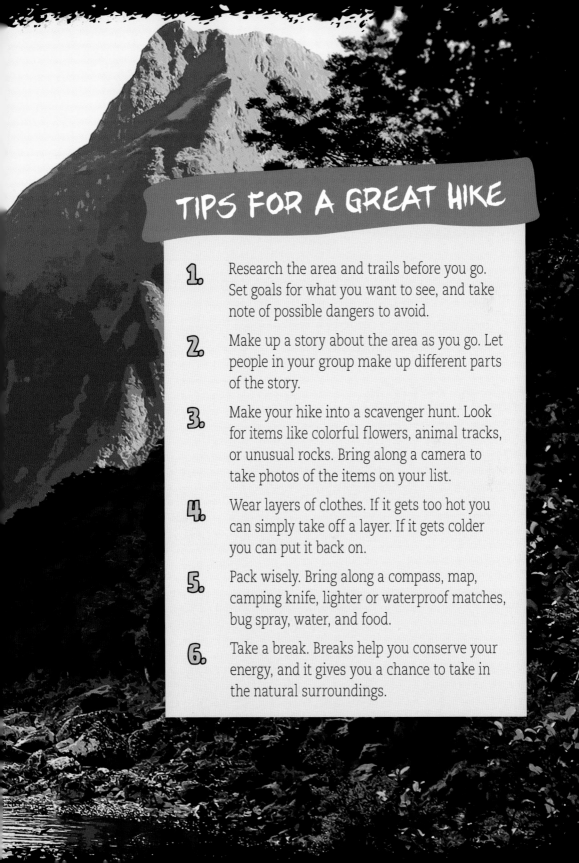

TIPS FOR A GREAT HIKE

1. Research the area and trails before you go. Set goals for what you want to see, and take note of possible dangers to avoid.

2. Make up a story about the area as you go. Let people in your group make up different parts of the story.

3. Make your hike into a scavenger hunt. Look for items like colorful flowers, animal tracks, or unusual rocks. Bring along a camera to take photos of the items on your list.

4. Wear layers of clothes. If it gets too hot you can simply take off a layer. If it gets colder you can put it back on.

5. Pack wisely. Bring along a compass, map, camping knife, lighter or waterproof matches, bug spray, water, and food.

6. Take a break. Breaks help you conserve your energy, and it gives you a chance to take in the natural surroundings.

FIND YOUR WAY IF YOU'RE LOST

When adventuring in the wild, a compass can help you find your way. If you get lost without one, don't panic. Just use these easy methods to help you navigate to safety.

USE A STICK

On a sunny day, place a 3-foot (0.9-meter) stick straight up and down in the ground. Place a small rock at the tip of the stick's shadow. Wait about 15 minutes and place another rock at the shadow's tip again. Next, draw a line between the two rocks.

The first rock you placed represents west, and the second is east. The line between them points exactly east and west. Draw another straight line across the middle of the first. This line will point north and south.

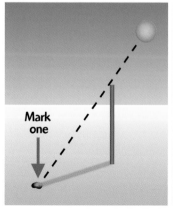

Mark one

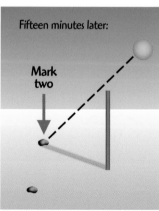

Fifteen minutes later:

Mark two

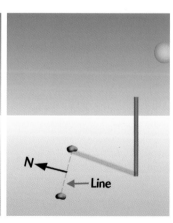

N

Line

USE A WATCH

You can find north and south using a analog (non-digital) watch. Point the hour hand directly toward the sun. Then draw an imaginary line midway between the hour hand and 12:00 on the watch. This line will point directly south. The opposite direction is north.

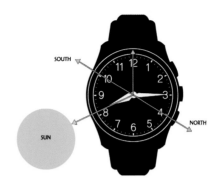

USE THE STARS

In the northern **hemisphere**, find the Big Dipper. Follow an imaginary line from the two stars at the front of the Big Dipper to a bright star a short distance away. This is the North Star, which is also the end of the handle of the Little Dipper. Look straight down from the North Star to the ground and you will be facing north.

In the southern hemisphere, find the Southern Cross **constellation**. Imagine a straight line extending out from the bottom of the cross. Below the cross are two bright stars. Imagine a second line extending from a point between the two stars. Note the point where the two lines meet. Look directly down from this point to the ground to find south.

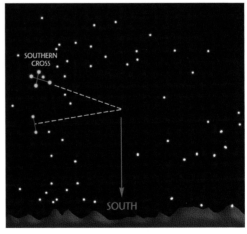

---

hemisphere—one half of the Earth

constellation—a group of stars that forms a shape

FIND WATER IN THE WILD

Getting lost in the wilderness can be a cold, lonely, and scary experience. If this happens to you, it's important to stay calm. Take a deep breath and get hold of your fear. The next thing you need to do is find water—you won't last long without it. People can live only a few days without water. Here are three ways to find water in the wild. They can be fun to practice even if your life is not in danger.

Collect Rainwater

Use a cup or bowl if you have it. If not, create a rain trap. Lay a plastic bag or rain jacket over a hole in the ground to form a crude bowl. Place rocks on the outer edges to hold the plastic in place.

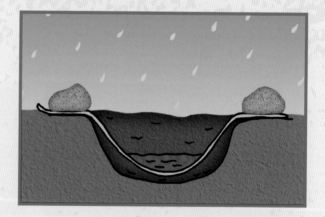

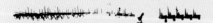

Collect Dew

Dew forms overnight as air temperatures cool. You can use a rain trap to collect the dew. Or you can soak it up from a grassy area with an absorbent cloth. Then just squeeze the water into a container.

Collect Condensation

Find a tree or plant with large leaves in a sunny area. Place a clear plastic bag over the leaves, and then tie the bag shut. Water will evaporate from the leaves and condense inside the bag. When there's enough water, simply remove the bag and drink the water or pour it into a container.

REMEMBER THE RULES OF THREE

THREE MINUTES: about how long you can survive without oxygen.

THREE HOURS: about how long you can survive without shelter in extremely hot or cold temperatures.

THREE DAYS: about how long you can survive without water.

THREE WEEKS: about how long you can survive without food.

**:** If you get lost, you might get hungry. But food should be the last of your worries! Water and shelter should be your first concern.

evaporate—to change from a liquid into a vapor or a gas

condense—to change from a gas to a liquid

EAT SOME PLANTS

If you're lost in the wild, you'll eventually need to eat. You'll improve your chances if you know about wildcrafting, or looking for food in the wild. But you need to be careful. Some berries and parts of plants might look tasty. But they could be poisonous. They may make you sick or even kill you. Generally, you should avoid plants that:

- **STINK**

- **ARE BRIGHTLY COLORED**

- **HAVE SPINES, FINE HAIR, OR THORNS**

These are nature's way of telling you to stay away. Don't eat any plant if you don't know what it is. If you plan to go exploring, get a guidebook to plants of the area ahead of time. Then if you get lost, you'll have clear information on what you can and cannot eat.

EDIBLE PLANTS		NON-EDIBLE PLANTS	
	Edible Berries (blackberries, raspberries, strawberries, blueberries)		Poisonous Berries (baneberry, belladonna, elderberry, nightshade, Jerusalem cherry)
	Edible Nuts (hickory nuts, acorns, pine nuts, beech nuts)		Poisonous Nuts (buckeye nuts, physic nuts)
	Wild Rice		Rosary Peas
	Cattail Roots		Hemlock
	Prickly Pear Cactus		Most Mushrooms

EAT SOME BUGS

It may sound gross, but you can eat many kinds of bugs and worms. Bugs have a lot of protein that can help keep you alive. Worms are usually found in cool, moist soil. Many bugs, such as ants, termites, or grubs can often be found under the bark of dead trees.

Like with plants, avoid bugs that are brightly colored or hairy, since they are likely poisonous. You also should avoid bugs that sting or bite, such as mosquitoes and bees, which could carry disease. You can eat some bugs raw. But if you can get a fire going, it's best to cook them first. Cooked bugs are safer to eat and are usually better tasting.

EDIBLE BUGS	NON-EDIBLE BUGS
1. Crickets	1. Fireflies
2. Grubs	2. Hairy or Spiky Caterpillars
3. Grasshoppers/Locusts	3. Blister Beetles
4. Termites	4. Flies
5. Ants and Eathworms	5. Ticks

TRUE ADVENTURE STORIES – PART I

An awesome trek into the wilderness is great, but there's rarely much risk involved. Even if you get lost, **Global Positioning System** (GPS) devices and cell phones can usually help you find your way. Sometimes you have to go out of your way to find true adventure. Here are a couple of stories about guys who created their own awesome life adventures.

THE ADVENTURE OF A LIFETIME

American Jeffrey Tayler felt like he needed a change in his life. Feeling the need for adventure, he quit his job and flew to Africa in 1995. There he bought a hand-carved canoe called a pirogue. With the help of just one African guide, Tayler paddled more than 1,000 miles (1,609 km) down the Congo River. Along the way he faced dangerous wild animals, scorching heat, powerful storms, and millions of biting insects.

In spite of the difficulties, Tayler said it was the greatest adventure of his life. He later wrote a book about his experiences called *Facing the Congo*.

Global Positioning System—an electronic tool used to find the location of an object

pirogue—a canoelike boat

SAILING SOLO

In 1999 Australian Jesse Martin finished an adventure that he began nearly a year before. He sailed all the way around the world in a 34-foot (10-meter) boat—by himself! During his journey he survived several severe storms, extreme temperatures, and terrible loneliness. That alone makes his story incredible. But he also set a record with his adventure. At just 18 years old, he became the youngest person to ever sail around the world alone.

Jesse recorded his journey with a video camera mounted on the boat. The footage was later used in a movie about his adventure called *Lionheart: The Jesse Martin Story*. Jesse's voyage took 328 days and covered more than 27,000 nautical miles (50,000 km).

nautical mile—a measure of distance at sea; one nautical mile equals 6,076 feet (1,852 m)

FIND EVIDENCE OF WILD ANIMALS

It can be difficult to spot wild animals. They usually stay hidden from humans. But you can learn which animals live in an area by observing the clues they leave behind. Look for their tracks in fresh snow, mud, or dirt. Watch for wild animal scat, or poop, that they leave in the woods. Some animals mark trees by chewing, scratching, or pecking on their trunks. And if you look closely, you may even spot their dens and nests while hiking in the wild.

SOME WILD ANIMAL SCAT:

Bear

Deer

Fox

Hare

Lynx

Moose

Raccoon

Wolf

Beaver

SOME ANIMALS AND THEIR TRACKS:

Deer

Mouse

Brown Bear

Hare

Beaver

Turkey

Fox

Hedgehog

Wolf

Badger

Lynx

Raccoon

Moose

Wild Boar

SURVIVE WILD ANIMAL ATTACKS — PART I

It's a wild world out there, but try to stay calm. Wild animal attacks are very rare. It's best to avoid dangerous animals in the wild. But if you do see one, keep your distance. Wild animals usually won't attack unless they feel threatened.

There is also safety in numbers, so hiking or camping in groups is a good idea. The following tips can help you to avoid or—if needed—survive an attack.

BEARS

With immense strength and razor-sharp teeth, bears can be deadly if they attack. Here are some tips for dealing with these powerful creatures if you meet them in the wild:

CARRY BEAR REPELLENT

These sprays do a good job of keeping bears away.

BACK AWAY SLOWLY

Don't run. Hold up your arms to make yourself look bigger. Make a lot of noise as you back off slowly.

USE WHATEVER YOU CAN

If the bear attacks, you'll need to defend yourself any way you can. Use a big rock or stick as a weapon. Go for the bear's sensitive areas, such as its eyes or nose.

MOUNTAIN LIONS

A mountain lion, or cougar, can be deadly—especially if it feels threatened. If you see one in the wild, don't run! Running will make the cat think you are prey. Follow these tips to survive a mountain lion attack:

DON'T PLAY DEAD

Acting dead just tells the cat you're helpless. Research shows that even standing still could trigger an attack.

MAKE YOURSELF LOOK BIGGER

Let the mountain lion know you're not to be messed with. Make loud noises and wave your arms around. Try to make yourself look larger and more threatening.

FIGHT BACK

If the cat still attacks you, you'll need to fight back. Use whatever weapons you can find, like sticks or rocks. Some people have even managed to fight off cougars with their bare hands.

AWESOME ATTACK ANIMALS

Wild animals have an amazing variety of attack styles. Here are a couple of the most unique styles found in nature.

BULLET ANTS

When threatened, these South American ants use powerful stingers to drive off an attacker. People who have been stung by them say it's so painful that it feels like being shot by a bullet.

ELECTRIC EELS

Zzzzzap! The electric eel can pump out up to 600 volts of electricity to stun its prey silly.

BUILD A SURVIVAL SHELTER

A survival shelter can protect you from rain, cold, and bugs. It can also provide shade on hot sunny days. Here's how to build a basic debris hut in the woods.

1. Pick a high spot where rain will flow away from your shelter. If possible, build your shelter near your supplies.

2. Find a straight branch that is 6 to 8 feet (1.8 to 2.4 m) long. This will be the **ridgepole** for the roof.

3. Prop up one end of the branch on a stump or forked tree. Set the other end on the ground.

4. Find several long, straight sticks. Set them against both sides of the ridgepole to form the ribs of the roof. Leave the high end open to form a doorway.

5. Next, lay several large leafy branches across the ribs to form the roof.

6. Now find a large amount of dry grass or leaves to use as **insulation**. Put about 2 feet (0.6 meter) of material on top of the roof. Add some more small branches on top to keep the insulation in place.

7. Finally, place more grass or leaves on the floor and in the doorway of the shelter. This will help hold your body heat inside.

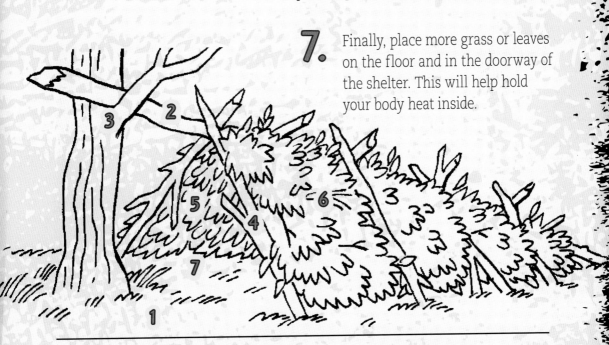

---

debris hut—a survival shelter designed to provide protection from bad weather and extreme temperatures

ridgepole—a beam along the ridge of a roof

insulation—a material that stops heat or cold from entering or escaping

BUILD A BAMBOO FISHING POLE

From advanced rods to electronic fish finders, modern fishing has become high-tech. But who needs fancy gear when you can make your own? Build this easy homemade fishing pole, and soon you'll be bringing in a great catch!

WHAT YOU'LL NEED:

- Pole: A 5-foot (1.5-m) piece of 3/4-inch (1.9-centimeter) bamboo from a garden shop.

- Line: You can use regular fishing line. But kite string also works well and is a lot cheaper.

- Fish Hooks: Size 6 or 8.

- Bobber: This floating marker helps you see when you've hooked a fish. You can buy a standard bobber at the store. Or you can just attach a piece of cork to your line with a rubber band.

- Sinkers: These weights help your hook and bait sink to where the fish are. Store-bought sinkers are easy to find. But you can also use simple washers or nuts.

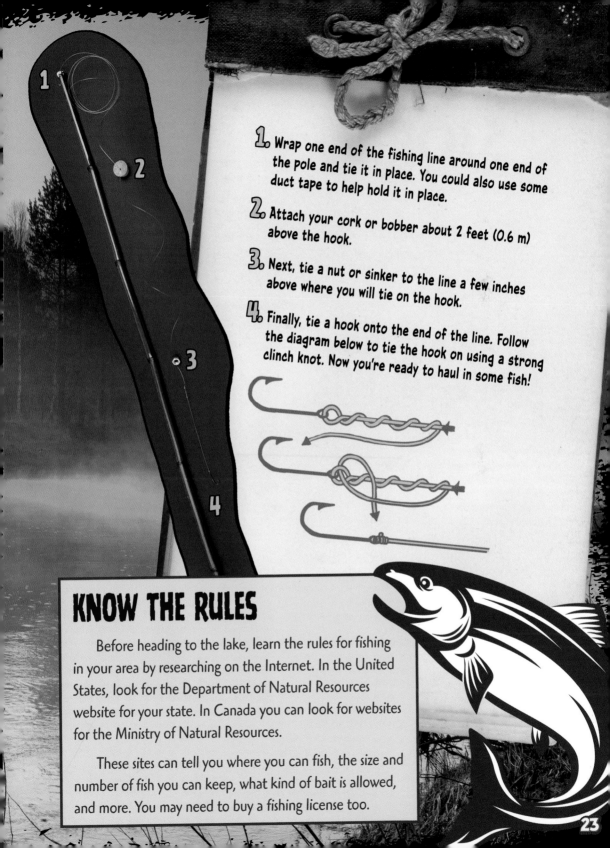

1. Wrap one end of the fishing line around one end of the pole and tie it in place. You could also use some duct tape to help hold it in place.

2. Attach your cork or bobber about 2 feet (0.6 m) above the hook.

3. Next, tie a nut or sinker to the line a few inches above where you will tie on the hook.

4. Finally, tie a hook onto the end of the line. Follow the diagram below to tie the hook on using a strong clinch knot. Now you're ready to haul in some fish!

KNOW THE RULES

Before heading to the lake, learn the rules for fishing in your area by researching on the Internet. In the United States, look for the Department of Natural Resources website for your state. In Canada you can look for websites for the Ministry of Natural Resources.

These sites can tell you where you can fish, the size and number of fish you can keep, what kind of bait is allowed, and more. You may need to buy a fishing license too.

TRUE ADVENTURE STORIES – PART II

History is filled with stories of men and women who have had incredible adventures. But kids have had some awesome adventures too. Here are a couple kids who could inspire even the hardiest adventurers.

CLIMBING THE SEVEN SUMMITS

As a boy Jordan Romero made an incredible goal for himself. He decided he would climb the highest mountain on each of the world's seven continents. Known as the "Seven Summits," nobody had climbed all of them at such a young age.

When he was 10 years old, Jordan climbed to the peak of Mt. Kilimanjaro in Africa. At age 13 he climbed the world's highest mountain, Mt. Everest in Tibet. Everest's peak is 29,035 feet (8,850 m) high, and Jordan was the youngest person ever to reach it. When he was 15, Jordan finished his goal by climbing to the peak of Mt. Vinson Massif in Antarctica.

Jordan set a record as the youngest person ever to conquer the Seven Summits. At the top of Vinson Massif, Jordan called his mom from a satellite phone to celebrate his amazing achievement.

ONE LONG HIKE

What's the longest walk you've ever taken? Omar Castillo Gallegos probably has you beat. It all started in 1985 when he was just 8 years old. Omar saw a TV show about the rain forests being destroyed in Mexico. He didn't like how animals' homes were being destroyed.

Omar wanted the Mexican government to protect the rain forest. So he decided to walk 800 miles (1,287 km) from his home in Mexico City to the rain forest to get the government's attention.

Omar's walk took 39 days and he wore out three pairs of shoes along the way. Omar soon gained a lot of attention. People began joining him for parts of his walk. It became like a parade. News stations began doing stories about him and his mission. In the end, Omar's long walk was worth it. Mexico's president promised to try to do what he could to help preserve Mexico's rain forests.

rain forest destruction in Mexico

rain forest—a thick forest or jungle where at least 100 inches (254 cm) of rain falls every year

ADVENTUROUS AUTHORS

Some of the world's greatest authors have also been awesome adventurers. Here are three guys who didn't just write amazing adventure stories. They were also tough as nails and great outdoorsmen themselves. Talk about these adventurers with your friends and decide who was the most awesome and adventurous author.

JACK LONDON

Books

London wrote more than 40 novels, including *White Fang*, *The Sea Wolf*, and *The Call of the Wild*.

Jobs

London worked as an oyster pirate, a sailor on a sealing ship, a war journalist, and a gold miner.

Great adventure

At age 17, he piloted the ship *Sophie Sutherland* through a typhoon off the coast of Japan.

Awesome quote

"The more difficult the feat, the greater the satisfaction at its accomplishment."

typhoon—a hurricane that forms in the Pacific Ocean

ERNEST HEMINGWAY

Books

Hemingway wrote 10 novels including *The Sun Also Rises*, *A Farewell to Arms*, *For Whom the Bell Tolls*, and *The Old Man and the Sea*. He also wrote several collections of short stories.

Jobs

Hemingway worked as an ambulance driver in World War I (1914–1918), a war journalist, a boxer, a big game hunter, and militia leader in World War II (1939–1945).

Great adventure

During World War I, Hemingway was severely wounded by mortar fire on July 8, 1918. In spite of his injuries, Hemingway managed to carry a fellow wounded soldier to safety.

Awesome quote

"Courage is grace under pressure."

SIR ARTHUR CONAN DOYLE

Books

Doyle wrote more than 25 novels and numerous short stories. But he's best known for his Sherlock Holmes books, including *The Adventures of Sherlock Holmes* and *The Hound of the Baskervilles*.

Jobs

Doyle worked as a sailor on a whaling ship, a ship's doctor, a body builder, a soccer goalie, and a criminal investigator.

Great adventure

When he was 20 years old, Doyle worked aboard the whaling ship *Hope* as the ship's surgeon. He often fell into the icy waters of the Arctic Ocean while helping crew members on the ship's deck.

Awesome quote

"There are heroisms all round us waiting to be done."

---

mortar—a short cannon that fires shells high in the air

criminal investigator—someone who studies a crime scene or a criminal case to find out how the crime was committed and who did it

SURVIVE WILD ANIMAL ATTACKS — PART II

RATTLESNAKE

They can be up to 8 feet (2.4 m) long. They can see in the dark. And they are **camouflaged**, so they are difficult to see in tall grass or under shrubs. They also have long, sharp fangs that inject deadly **venom**, and their strike is lightning quick. Follow these tips if you ever find yourself in rattlesnake country.

AVOID THEM

Know what rattlers look like, and be on the lookout. Don't reach into places where snakes like to hide, such as piles of rocks or sticks. Listen for their warning rattling sound. Wear boots, long pants, and thick socks for protection in case they do try to bite.

GET AWAY

If you see a snake—freeze. Then back away slowly until you're at least 6 to 8 feet (1.8 to 2.4 m) away. Then run!

TREAT BITE WOUNDS

Don't try to cut open the wound and suck out the poison. That's just for the movies. Instead, keep the bite below heart level and don't move around too much. Movement makes the poison spread more quickly through your body. Call 911 right away.

camouflage—a pattern or color on an animal's skin that makes it blend in with the things around it

venom—a poisonous liquid produced by some animals

SKUNK

Skunks normally won't attack you. But if they feel threatened, they'll defend themselves with a nasty spray.

BE COOL

If you see a skunk, don't threaten it. Stand still or walk away.

KNOW WHEN TO RUN

If the skunk starts to stomp its feet or turns its rear end toward you, run! Skunk spray can cause nausea, coughing, shortness of breath, and even temporary blindness.

DEODORIZE

If you do get sprayed, you'll need to neutralize it. Mix together 1 quart (0.9 liter) of hydrogen peroxide, 1/4 cup (60 mL) of baking soda, and 1 teaspoon (5 mL) of mild dishwashing soap. Then wash yourself all over with the mixture. You might need to do it more than once.

ALLIGATORS AND CROCODILES

If you're stuck in a swamp and see a 12 foot (3.7 meter) alligator swimming your way—run! Alligators and crocodiles have the most powerful jaws of any living creature. Scientists think a large crocodile's bite force is about the same as the mighty Tyrannosaurus rex once had. If one bites you, you're in serious trouble.

But not all hope is lost. These animals can move only about 10 miles (16 km) per hour for a short distance. If one comes at you, run away at full speed. You should be able to get away.

If running isn't an option, there's another defense you can try. These reptiles' jaws are powerful when biting down, but they are very weak when opening. If necessary, try to get your arms around the animal's snout. You should be able to hold its jaws shut until it gives up—just don't let go!

GLOSSARY

camouflage (KAM-uh-flahzh)—a pattern or color on an animal's skin that helps it blend in with the things around it

condense (kuhn-DENS)—to change from a gas to a liquid

constellation (kahn-stuh-LAY-shuhn)—a group of stars that forms a shape

criminal investigator (KRIM-uh-nuhl in-VESS-tuh-gate-ur)—someone who studies a crime scene or a criminal case to find out how the crime was committed and who did it

debris hut (duh-BREE HUT)—a survival shelter designed to provide protection from bad weather and extreme temperatures

evaporate (i-VA-puh-rayt)—to change from a liquid into a vapor or a gas

forage (FOR-ij)—to search for food

Global Positioning System (GLOH-buhl puh-ZI-shuh-ning SISS-tuhm)—an electronic tool used to find the location of an object

hemisphere (HEM-uhss-fihr)—one half of the Earth

insulation (in-suh-LAY-shuhn)—a material that stops heat or cold from entering or escaping

mortar (MOR-tur)—a short cannon that fires shells high in the air

nautical mile (NAW-tik-uhl MILE)—a measure of distance at sea; one nautical mile equals 6,076 feet (1,852 m)

pirogue (PEE-rohg)—a canoelike boat

rain forest (RAYN FOR-ist)—a thick forest or jungle where at least 100 inches (254 cm) of rain falls every year

ridgepole (RIJ-pohl)—a beam along the ridge of a roof

typhoon (tie-FOON)—a hurricane that forms in the western Pacific Ocean

venom (VEN-uhm)—a poisonous liquid produced by some animals

READ MORE

Howard, Melanie A. *Camping for Kids.* Into the Great Outdoors. North Mankato, Minn.: Capstone Press, 2013.

Hurley, Michael. *Surviving the Wilderness.* Extreme Survival. Chicago: Raintree, 2011.

Lecreux, Michele. *The Boys' Book of Adventure.* Hauppauge, N.Y.: Barrons Educational Series, Inc., 2013.

INTERNET SITES

FactHound offers a safe, fun way to find Internet sites related to this book. All of the sites on FactHound have been researched by our staff.

Here's all you do:

Visit www.facthound.com

Type in this code: 9781476539225

Check out projects, games and lots more at
www.capstonekids.com